T0288631

Earth

Richard Northcott

OXFORD
UNIVERSITY PRESS

OXFORD
UNIVERSITY PRESS

Great Clarendon Street, Oxford, OX2 6DP, United Kingdom

Oxford University Press is a department of the University of Oxford. It furthers the University's objective of excellence in research, scholarship, and education by publishing worldwide. Oxford is a registered trade mark of Oxford University Press in the UK and in certain other countries

ISBN: 978 0 19 464679 6

An Audio Pack containing this book and an Audio download is also available, ISBN 978 0 19 402157 9

This book is also available as an e-Book, ISBN 978 0 19 410858 4.

An accompanying Activity Book is also available, ISBN 978 0 19 464669 7

Printed in China

This book is printed on paper from certified and well-managed sources.

ACKNOWLEDGEMENTS

Illustrations by: Kelly Kennedy pp.5 (earth and sun), 10, 11, 12, 16, 19, 26; Mark Ruffle p.5 (map); Alan Rowe pp.20, 22, 24, 28, 30, 32, 35, 38, 39.

The Publishers would also like to thank the following for their kind permission to reproduce photographs and other copyright material: Alamy pp.13 (Malcolm Schuyl/penguins), 14 (Eitan Simanor), 15 (Jan Carroll/rainforest), 17 (Martin Borrovsky/INSADCO Photography); Corbis pp.4 (Kulka), 6 (Frank Krahmer), 7 (Tadao Yamamoto/amanaimages/cliffs, Robert Postma/First Light/Colca Canyon), 9 (WIN-Images/rough sea), 16 (Martin Rietze/Westend61), 18 (David Fleetham/Visuals Unlimited/jellyfish); Getty Images pp.9 (Panoramic Images/calm ocean), 12 (Wally Herbert/Robert Harding World Imagery); Naturepl.com pp.15 (Nick Garbutt/pitcher plant), 18 (Georgette Douwma/underwater); Oxford University Press p.3; Photolibrary pp.8 (Tibor Bognar/Photononstop), 10 (SGM SGM), 11 (Mike Kipling/The Travel Library), 13 (Calvin W Hall/Alaskastock/Northern Lights).

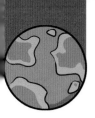 # Introduction

Let's look at Earth. Let's look at oceans and rivers, mountains and forests. Earth is amazing, and it has lots of amazing places.

Where is it hot on Earth?
Where is it cold on Earth?
Where can we find water on Earth?

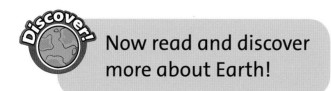 Now read and discover more about Earth!

clouds

land

water

We're in space and we're looking at Earth. What can we see? We can see many colors. We can see land, water, and clouds.

Earth is a planet. There are many, many planets in space, but there's only one Earth. Earth is our home. Millions of plants, animals, and people live here.

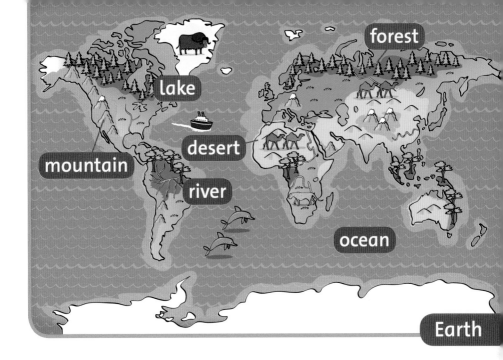

forest

lake

mountain

desert

river

ocean

Earth

On the land, there are forests, mountains, and deserts. Most of Earth's water is in oceans, but there's water in lakes and rivers, too.

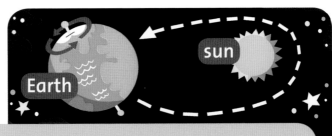

sun

Earth

Discover!

Earth goes around the sun every year. Earth also turns every day.

→ Go to pages 20–21 for activities.

2 Land

We live on the land. The land is under our feet. The land can be snowy mountains or green valleys. It can be forests or deserts.

These mountains are in China. Next to the mountains, there are valleys. The mountains and valleys on Earth are millions of years old.

Mountains in China

cliff

Cliffs in Australia

The land can fall into the ocean and make cliffs. These amazing cliffs are in Australia.

Rivers can make deep valleys in the land. These deep valleys are called canyons. Look at this amazing canyon in Peru. It's called the Colca Canyon.

The Colca Canyon

→ Go to pages 22–23 for activities.

3 Water

On Earth, there's water in rivers, lakes, and oceans.

Most rivers come from mountains. Snow falls on the mountains. The snow melts and the water goes down the mountains. Rain falls, then more water goes into the rivers. Most rivers go to the ocean.

When a river comes to a cliff, it makes a waterfall. Niagara Falls are amazing waterfalls in Canada and the USA.

Niagara Falls

A Calm Ocean

When the ocean is calm, the waves are small. People can swim in the ocean when it's calm.

In bad weather, the ocean can be rough. The wind makes big waves. People can't swim in the ocean when it's rough.

A Rough Ocean

→ Go to pages 24–25 for activities.

4 Hot Places

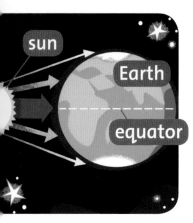

A lot of hot places on Earth are near the equator. Near the equator, the light from the sun is strong. It's often hot in summer and in winter.

There are many hot deserts near the equator.

A Hot Desert

Monument Valley

Monument Valley is in a desert in the USA. It's very hot and sunny there. There are weeks and months with no rain.

In some very hot places in summer, there's no water in the rivers. Plants and fish can't live there.

hole

Discover!

When it's hot, the lungfish makes a hole in the soil. It can live there with no water!

→ Go to pages 26–27 for activities.

5 Cold Places

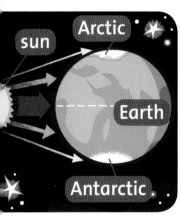

The Arctic and the Antarctic are very cold places. In the Arctic and the Antarctic, the light from the sun is weak. Winter is very long. It's dark for six months!

In the Arctic, there's lots of deep snow. People can't drive their cars in the snow, so they use sleds and dogs.

In the Arctic

sled

penguin

There's lots of snow in the Antarctic, too. Penguins live in the Antarctic. When it's very cold, they stand near their friends, so they are not cold.

Discover!

In the Arctic and the Antarctic, electricity from the sun makes amazing colors in the sky.

Go to pages 28–29 for activities.

6 Wet Places

Do you like cold, rainy days? In some places, there are lots of rainy days. Rain isn't always cold. Rain often comes with hot weather.

In India, there's lots of rain in hot weather. It's rainy there from June to September. People go everywhere with an umbrella. The rainy time in India is called the monsoon.

In the Monsoon

In a Rainforest

It's very wet in rainforests, too. It's often hot and rainy. Many amazing animals and plants live in rainforests.

This rainforest plant can eat insects!

Go to pages 30–31 for activities.

Under the Land

soil

rock

hot rock

Let's look at the land. What can we see? We can see soil. Plants live in soil and they find water there. Under the soil, there's rock. Rock is millions of years old.

Deep in Earth, the rock is very, very hot. When a volcano erupts, hot rock comes out. People and animals run. They are scared.

A Volcano Erupting

There's water under the land, too. The water can make caves. You can see amazing rock in caves.

These caves are in Slovenia. They're called the Skocjan Caves.

In the Skocjan Caves, the river goes under the land for 34 kilometers.

Go to pages 32–33 for activities.

8 In the Ocean

The ocean is an amazing place.
There are millions of fish and plants
in the ocean.

Discover!

It's dark in the deep ocean.
Some animals make light
so they can see in the dark.

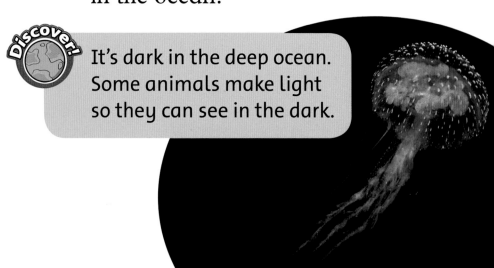

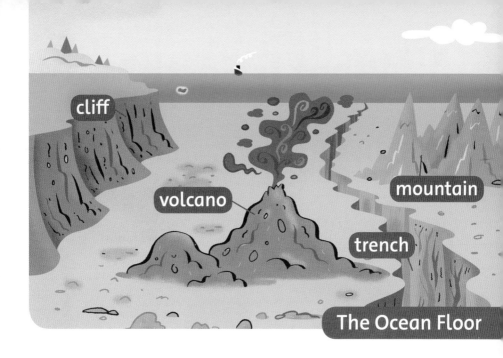

cliff

volcano

mountain

trench

The Ocean Floor

Do you know there are cliffs, mountains, and volcanoes in the ocean? There are long, deep canyons, too. They are called trenches. They are in the ocean floor.

The deep ocean is cold and dark. We can't swim there. We can't see the ocean floor. With new cameras, we can learn more about the deep ocean. Every day we learn new things about Earth.

→ Go to pages 34–35 for activities.

1 What Is Earth?

← Read pages 4–5.

1 Write the words.

> desert   river   mountain
> ocean   cloud   forest

1 ___ocean___   2 _____   3 _____

4 _____   5 _____   6 _____

2 Circle the correct words.

1 Earth is a **space** / (**planet.**)

2 There are many planets in **space** / **Earth.**

3 There's **millions** / **water** on Earth.

4 Most of Earth's water is in **oceans** / **forests.**

3 Complete the sentences.

day goes ~~takes~~ land one

1 There are rivers and __lakes__ on Earth.

2 On the _____, there are mountains and deserts.

3 Earth turns every _____ .

4 Earth _____ around the sun every year.

5 There's only _____ Earth.

4 Match. Then write the sentences.

On Earth, there's	in lakes and rivers.
There's water	is our home.
Earth is a	land and water.
Millions of people	live on Earth.
Earth	planet.

1 __On Earth, there's land and water.__

2 _____

3 _____

4 _____

5 _____

2 Land

← Read pages 6–7.

1 Write the words. Then match.

1 sfcfli

   <u>cliffs</u>

2 aldn

   _____

3 alyvle

   _____

4 aoynnc

   _____

2 Find and write the words.

mountainmillionsamazingoceansnowyforest

1 <u>mountain</u>   3 _____   5 _____

2 _____   4 _____   6 _____

3 Circle the correct words.

1 We **live** / **ocean** on the land.

2 The land can be **mountains** / **millions** or valleys.

3 A **mountain** / **canyon** is a deep valley.

4 The mountains and valleys on Earth **aren't** / **are** very old.

5 The land can **fall** / **make** into the ocean.

4 Complete the sentences.

1 The land is ___under our feet___ .
   (feet / under / our)

2 The land can _____ .
   (snowy / mountains / be)

3 Rivers can _____ .
   (valleys / deep / make)

4 A canyon is _____ .
   (valley / a / deep)

5 There's a _____ .
   (Peru / in / canyon)

6 The mountains on _____ .
   (old / Earth / are)

③ Water

← Read pages 8–9.

1 Complete the puzzle.

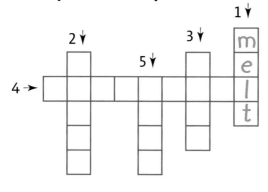

1 ↓
2 ↓
3 ↓
5 ↓
4 →

m
e
l
t

2 Write *true* or *false*.

1 There's water in rivers. _true_

2 Most rivers come from oceans. _____

3 Rain falls, then more water goes
into rivers. _____

4 Most rivers go to the ocean. _____

5 When the ocean is calm, the waves
are big. _____

6 People can swim in the ocean when
it's rough. _____

3 Complete the sentences.

cliff   oceans   swim   wind

1 When a river comes to a _____ , it makes a waterfall.

2 There's water in rivers, lakes, and _____ .

3 In bad weather, the _____ makes big waves in the ocean.

4 You can't _____ in the ocean when it's rough.

4 Answer the questions.

1 Where is there water on Earth?

   On Earth, there's water in rivers,
   lakes, and oceans.

2 Where do most rivers come from?

   _____

3 Where do most rivers go?

   _____

4 What does a river make when it comes to a cliff?

   _____

④ Hot Places

← Read pages 10–11.

1 Write the words.

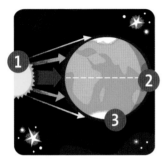

equator   Earth   sun

1 _____

2 _____

3 _____

2 Circle the correct words.

1 Near the equator, it's often **summer** / **hot** in winter.

2 There are many hot **deserts** / **strong** near the equator.

3 When there's no **desert** / **water**, the lungfish lives in a hole.

4 Fish can't live in **plants** / **rivers** with no water.

5 It's very hot and **sunny** / **cold** in Monument Valley.

3 Match.

1 There are a lot of	the light from the sun is strong.
2 Monument Valley is	lungfish makes a hole in the soil.
3 It's hot and	sunny in Monument Valley.
4 When it's hot, the	in the USA.
5 Near the equator,	hot places near the equator.

4 Answer the questions.

1 Where are there a lot of hot places on Earth?

_____

2 Where is Monument Valley?

_____

3 How is the weather in Monument Valley?

_____

4 What does the lungfish do when it's hot?

_____

5 Cold Places

← Read pages 12–13.

1 Write the words.

dog   electricity
penguin   sled

1 _____

2 _____

3 _____

4 _____

2 Circle the correct words.

1 The Arctic is a **cold** / **hot** place.

2 There's **lots of** / **no** snow in the Arctic.

3 In the Antarctic, it's **hot** / **dark** for six months.

4 In the Arctic, people **can't** / **can** drive their cars in deep snow.

5 Penguins live in the **Antarctic** / **Arctic**.

6 Penguins stand near their **sleds** / **friends**.

3 Complete the sentences.

cold   colors   snow   stand   sun   winter

1 It's very _____ in the Arctic and the
   Antarctic.

2 In the Arctic and the Antarctic, the light from
   the _____ is weak.

3 In the Arctic, the _____ is very deep.

4 In the Arctic and the Antarctic, _____
   is very long.

5 When it's very cold, penguins _____
   near their friends.

6 Electricity from the sun makes amazing
   _____ in the sky.

4 Match.

1 In the Arctic,
   people have

2 In the Antarctic,

3 The Arctic and the
   Antarctic

4 Electricity from
   the sun makes

amazing colors
in the sky.

there are penguins.

are very cold places.

sleds and dogs.

6 Wet Places

← Read pages 14–15.

1 Write the words. Then match.

1 faiersontr

_____

2 sltnap

_____

3 beualrml

_____

4 nctessi

_____

2 Find and write the words.

coldrainyhotweathermonsoonsummer

1 _____   3 _____   5 _____

2 _____   4 _____   6 _____

3 Circle the correct words.

1 Rain **is** / **isn't** always cold.

2 In India, it's **rainy** / **sunny** from June to September.

3 In India, the rainy time is called the **weather** / **monsoon**.

4 Rainforests are **water** / **wet** places.

5 There are flowers in **umbrellas** / **rainforests**.

6 There **are** / **aren't** amazing plants in rainforests.

4 Complete the sentences.

1 The monsoon _____ .
   (rainy / time / the / is)

2 It's often hot _____ .
   (rainforests / in / rainy / and)

3 There are amazing _____ .
   (in / animals / rainforests)

4 One rainforest plant _____ .
   (eat / can / insects)

7 Under the Land

← Read pages 16–17.

1 Complete the puzzle.

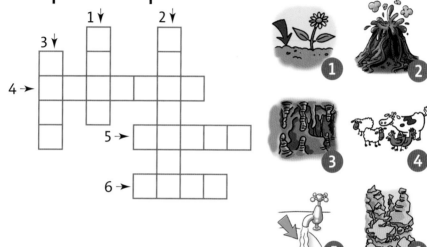

2 Write *true* or *false*.

1 You can't see soil on the land. _____

2 Plants live in soil. _____

3 Deep in Earth, the rock is very cold. _____

4 Water can make caves. _____

5 You can see amazing rock in caves. _____

6 There are caves in Slovenia. _____

3 Complete the sentences.

caves   find   volcano   people   rock   Water

1 Plants _____ water in soil.

2 The _____ under the land is very old.

3 When a _____ erupts, hot rock comes out.

4 When a volcano erupts, _____ are scared.

5 _____ under the land can make caves.

6 You can see amazing rock in _____ .

4 Answer the questions.

1 What is under the soil?

_____

2 How old is rock?

_____

3 What comes out when a volcano erupts?

_____

4 What can you see in caves?

_____

8 In the Ocean

← Read pages 18–19.

1 Circle the correct words.

1 The ocean is an amazing **mountain** / **place**.

2 There are millions of **fish** / **people** in the ocean.

3 Some **animals** / **millions** live in the deep ocean.

4 There **are** / **aren't** cliffs and mountains in the ocean.

5 It's **light** / **dark** in the deep ocean.

6 Every day we learn **new** / **old** things about Earth.

2 Match.

1 There are millions of
2 Trenches are
3 Some animals
4 It's very cold and

long, deep canyons.
dark in the deep ocean.
plants in the ocean.
make light.

3 Answer the questions.

1 What are trenches?

_____

2 Is it hot or cold in the deep ocean?

_____

4 Complete the puzzle. Find the secret words.

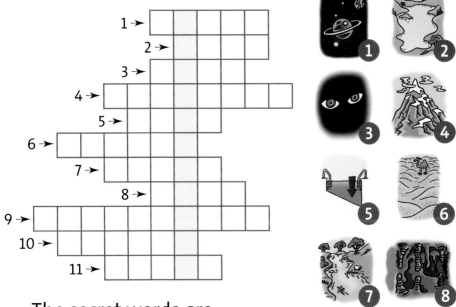

1 →
2 →
3 →
4 →
5 →
6 →
7 →
8 →
9 →
10 →
11 →

The secret words are:

P
E

My Country Poster

1 Complete the chart. Write the names of places, animals, and plants in your country.

In My Country	
A River	A Lake
_____	_____
A Mountain	A Forest
_____	_____
Animals	Plants
_____	_____
_____	_____
_____	_____

2 Make a poster. Find or draw pictures of the places, animals, and plants. Write their names.

3 Display your poster.

Information Cards

1 Complete the information cards about amazing places on Earth.

Place	Colca Canyon
What is it?	It's a canyon.
Where is it?	It's in Peru.

Place	
What is it?	
Where is it?	

Place	
What is it?	
Where is it?	

2 Make more information cards about amazing places on Earth.

3 Display your information cards.

Picture Dictionary

cave

cliffs

cloud

dark

deep

desert

down

Earth

electricity

fall

forest

insects

lake

land

light

melt

million

mountain

near

ocean

planet

plants

rainforest

river

rock

soil

space

valley

volcano

water

waterfall

waves

Oxford Read and Discover

Discover!

Series Editor: Hazel Geatches • CLIL Adviser: John Clegg

Oxford Read and Discover graded readers are at six levels, for students from age 6 and older. They cover many topics within three subject areas, and support English across the curriculum, or Content and Language Integrated Learning (CLIL).

Available for each reader:
• Audio Pack
• Activity Book

Available for selected readers:
• e-Books

Teaching notes & CLIL guidance: **www.oup.com/elt/teacher/readanddiscover**

Subject Area / Level	The World of Science & Technology	The Natural World	The World of Arts & Social Studies
1 — 300 headwords	• Eyes • Fruit • Trees • Wheels	• At the Beach • In the Sky • Wild Cats • Young Animals	• Art • Schools
2 — 450 headwords	• Electricity • Plastic • Sunny and Rainy • Your Body	• Camouflage • Earth • Farms • In the Mountains	• Cities • Jobs
3 — 600 headwords	• How We Make Products • Sound and Music • Super Structures • Your Five Senses	• Amazing Minibeasts • Animals in the Air • Life in Rainforests • Wonderful Water	• Festivals Around the World • Free Time Around the World
4 — 750 headwords	• All About Plants • How to Stay Healthy • Machines Then and Now • Why We Recycle	• All About Desert Life • All About Ocean Life • Animals at Night • Incredible Earth	• Animals in Art • Wonders of the Past
5 — 900 headwords	• Materials to Products • Medicine Then and Now • Transportation Then and Now • Wild Weather	• All About Islands • Animal Life Cycles • Exploring Our World • Great Migrations	• Homes Around the World • Our World in Art
6 — 1,050 headwords	• Cells and Microbes • Clothes Then and Now • Incredible Energy • Your Amazing Body	• All About Space • Caring for Our Planet • Earth Then and Now • Wonderful Ecosystems	• Food Around the World • Helping Around the World